PREPARE HIM ROOM

28 WAYS TO EMBRACE THE SPIRIT OF CHRISTMAS

Prepare Him Room: 28 Ways to Embrace the Spirit of Christmas

Publisher:
Time-Warp Wife Ministries
114 Wyndham Estate Drive Steinbach, Manitoba
R5G 2K6

Interior design by Darlene Schacht Cover design by Darlene Schacht
Some images from Adobe Stock Photo

ISBN 978-1-988984-28-5

PREPARE HIM ROOM

28 WAYS TO EMBRACE THE SPIRIT OF CHRISTMAS

Darlene Schacht

Time-Warp Wife Ministries

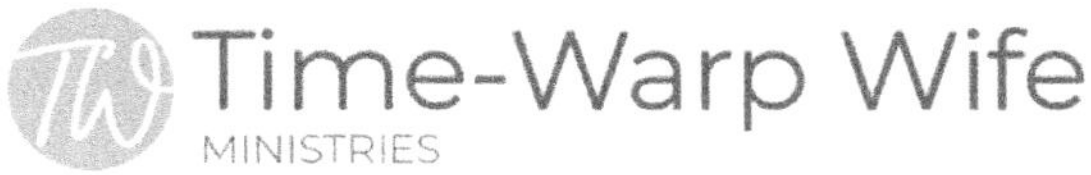

Table of Contents

You Might Also Like:

Unlike many traditional Advent books that prompt us to focus on ourselves, Quieting Your Heart directs our attention to the heart of the matter—God's word. Cutting through the noise of commercials, crowds, and cash register bells, we're pausing to listen intently to what God has to say.

Immerse yourself in rich biblical themes of Love, Joy, Hope, and Peace through this devotional Bible study. Each day presents Scripture and an article that thoughtfully highlights the text, centering the study on the character of God and the richness He brings to our lives.

Available at Amazon.

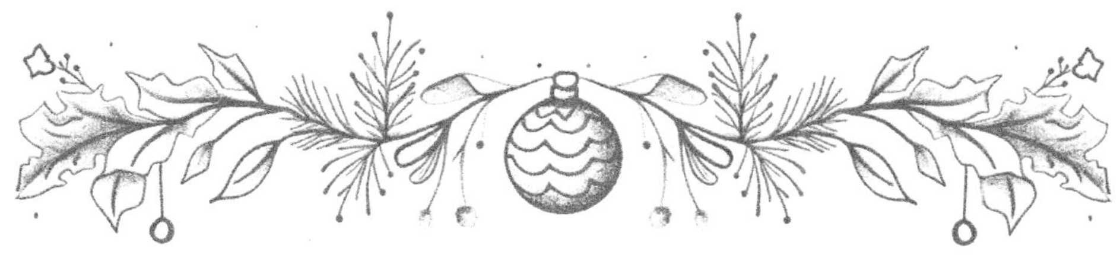

Embrace the Spirit of Christmas

*For to us a child is born, to us a son is given, and the government will be
on his shoulders. And he will be called Wonderful Counselor,
Mighty God, Everlasting Father, Prince of Peace.*
—*Isaiah 9:6*

Hi Besties,

Have you ever felt overwhelmed by the pressures of Christmas? Wishing you could go back to a simpler time, when the season was more about joy and less about stress? I think many of us can relate. If we're not careful, the holidays—with all the expectations, to-do lists, bells, whistles, hustle, and bustle—can overshadow the true reason we celebrate.

When I think back to Christmas days long ago, I can't help but think of my mom. She had an incredible ability to make every Christmas feel special. Weeks of preparation went into decorating, shopping, cooking, baking, cleaning, and wrapping gifts—all to create a home filled with comfort and joy during the holiday season. Our freezer was packed with homemade treats—sugar cookies, shortbread, peanut butter cookies, butter tarts, you name it. She filled every table with festive candies, nuts, and those little Japanese oranges that somehow made Christmas complete.

As I tried to follow in her footsteps, I found myself overwhelmed. She was so good at it, and it came naturally to her, but perfection is not my forte—especially when it comes to baking.

It took me a while to learn to let go. To release the expectations, the pursuit of perfection, and the frustration that came with it. Christmas is meant to be a time of hope, peace, joy, and love. It's about celebrating the birth of Jesus, not about achieving a perfect holiday scene. That's what this book is about. It's not about adding more tasks to your to-do list; it's about making room—preparing Him room—in our hearts and in our homes. It's about focusing on what truly matters, finding contentment, and nurturing the relationships that bring meaning to our lives.

I invite you, as you read these pages, to pause. Breathe. Let go of the pressure to create a perfect Christmas and instead embrace its true spirit. Let's take this journey together, finding comfort in knowing that we don't need to do it all—just make room for Him.

As you read, I encourage you to ask yourself: What would Christmas look like if I let go of the expectations and truly embraced its spirit?

We're all in this together—seeking hope, peace, joy, and love in a sometimes chaotic world. Let's walk this path side by side.

May you truly feel the love and peace of Jesus this Christmas, no matter what else is going on around you.

Darlene Schacht,
The Time-Warp Wife

Christmas isn't about the perfection of our homes, but the preparation of our hearts. It's the quiet moments, the small gestures of love, and the warmth of His presence that make the season truly meaningful.

Darlene Schacht

THE FOUR ADVENT CANDLES are a beautiful Christmas tradition. Each one has a special meaning, reminding us to prepare our hearts for the coming celebration. Typically, one candle is lit for each of the four Sundays leading up to Christmas. Maybe you'd like to do the same throughout the 4 weeks of our study.

1. **The First Candle: The Candle of Hope**

    This candle is all about hope and anticipation. It's often called the Prophecy Candle because it represents the promises of the Old Testament about the coming of the Messiah. When we light it, we remember the long-awaited promise of our Savior and the hope God brings to a world that can sometimes feel dark.

2. **The Second Candle: The Candle of Peace**
    The second candle stands for peace. It's also known as the Bethlehem Candle, named after the place where Jesus was born. This candle reminds us that Jesus brought peace into the world— peace between God and humanity. It's a comforting reminder that through Him, we're reconciled to God.

3. **The Third Candle: The Candle of Joy**
    This candle symbolizes joy and is sometimes called the Shepherd's Candle. It takes us back to that moment when the shepherds heard the incredible news of Christ's birth from the angels—how joyful they must have been! This candle is pink, a little different from the others, to show a break in the more reflective tone of the season, and instead focus on the joy that Jesus brings.

4. **The Fourth Candle: The Candle of Love**
    The fourth candle represents love and is often called the Angel's Candle. It's all about remembering the love of God for us—shown so beautifully in the gift of His Son, Jesus. The angels proclaimed this message of love and peace to the world on the night of Jesus' birth, and we carry that message in our hearts today.

Embracing
Hope

Day 1

Trust in God's Plan

"For my thoughts are not your thoughts, neither are your ways my ways,"
declares the Lord. "As the heavens are higher than the earth,
so are my ways higher than your ways and my thoughts
than your thoughts." —Isaiah 55:8-9, NIV

Read: Luke 1-2

When my kids were younger, one of our favorite Christmas traditions was setting up the nativity scene. Gathered around the big box of decorations, excitement filled the air as little hands eagerly unwrapped each figure—Mary, Joseph, the shepherds, the animals, and of course, baby Jesus. Each piece was handled with excitement and care.

One year, as we unpacked the nativity set, we realized something was missing—baby Jesus. We searched everywhere, digging through tissue paper and old ornaments, checking the box again and again. The kids even crawled under the tree, hoping He had just rolled away. But He wasn't there. The whole nativity scene felt incomplete without Him. Mary and Joseph were there, the shepherds were there, but without Jesus, the heart of the message was missing.

That moment made me realize how true this is for our lives. We can have all the right pieces—the job, the house, the family, even a church—but without Jesus at the center, none of it feels right. There's an emptiness that nothing else can fill. That year, we found a small doll from the toy bin to use as a stand-in for baby Jesus. It worked in a pinch, but it was a clear reminder—when we lose sight of Jesus, nothing else can quite fill His place.

As I got to thinking about the gap in our nativity scene, I realized how easy it is to lose sight of Jesus amid the busyness of life, especially at Christmas. There's always one more gift to buy, one more event to attend, and it's so easy to forget Who we're celebrating and why. How we try to fill the empty spaces in our lives with other things, hoping they'll bring us peace. But the truth is, nothing else could ever take His place.

Think about the first Christmas. God's plan for the birth of His Son was far from what anyone expected. A young, unmarried girl, a simple, uncomfortable stable. It was messy and humble. But God's plans are always perfect, even when they unfold in unconventional ways. Mary and Joseph didn't know how everything would play out. They couldn't see the whole picture, but they chose to trust. Because they did, the Savior of the world was born in that little stable, bringing light to the world.

This Christmas, if you find yourself feeling like something's amiss, if life isn't fitting together the way that you planned, take a step back. Remember that Jesus fills every gap, every longing, every empty place in our heart. God's plans may not turn out the way we hope or expect, but His wisdom is far greater than ours, and His grace is sufficient for us.

Let's choose to trust Him, even when the way seems unclear, or the pieces don't fit in the way we expect. His presence fills what's lacking, and with Him, we find true meaning and wholeness. This Christmas, let's invite Him in—not just into our homes but into every moment and every plan. Because when Jesus is at the center of our lives, everything else falls into place.

Today's Challenge:

Take one small step in faith today, even if you can't see the full picture. Whether it's reaching out to someone, tackling an unfamiliar task, or letting go of a worry, trust that God will guide your path.

Throughout history God has redirected the paths of His people in unexpected ways. Can you think of one? And how might this encourage you in difficult times?

Can you remember a time when God blessed you with a surprising detour? What happened?

Day 2

Seek Contentment

I know what it is to be in need, and I know what it is to have plenty.
I have learned the secret of being content in any and every situation, whether
well fed or hungry, whether living in plenty or in want.
—Philippians 4:12, NIV

Read: Psalm 23

I want everything to go well for my family at Christmas—whether it's hoping the turkey will be cooked in time, the food will taste good, or the wrapping will all get done before midnight. I pray things will fall into place. I hope that my kids will have a good day—don't we all?

But here's the thing—what happens when things don't fall into place? When the turkey is dry, the mashed potatoes are lumpy, and you forgot to pick up that last gift? What do we do when our picture-perfect Christmas unravels?

The truth is, Christmas isn't meant to be picture-perfect. It's meant to remind us of Christ. If we think that first night was calm and serene, and everything went as planned, we're sorely mistaken. Imagine being nine months pregnant, traveling 85 miles of rough terrain on a donkey, only to find out there's no room at the inn. Imagine going into labor with no proper bed or blanket in sight. There was no one boiling water or calling a doctor like we see on TV. It was just Mary, Joseph, and the uncertainty of that night. And maybe a little boy playing drums—okay, maybe not, but you get the idea.

Maybe that's your life today, in one way or another. The picture-perfect marriage you dreamed of is filled with challenges you never saw coming.

The kids you hoped would always be close have distanced themselves. The cozy home you envisioned is too costly to fix. How can we be content when this world keeps letting us down?

There's a common mindset that says, "When my circumstances change, I'll be happy." But the truth is, if we're not happy with less, we won't be happy with more. Paul offers us a better way of living, removing the crutch we're so used to leaning on. He writes, "I have learned the secret of being content in any and every situation, whether well fed or hungry, whether living in plenty or in want" (Philippians 4:12, NIV).

Paul's secret has nothing to do with the changing world around him—it's about the Spirit living within him. Throughout Scripture, we see God's people thriving in difficult moments, not because God is reshaping their circumstances, but because He's reshaping their hearts.

A change of heart leads to a change in attitude—one of gratitude. Just as Paul "learned" the secret of being content, we too can learn to live that way, with the help of the Holy Spirit. So, this Christmas, instead of focusing on what we don't have, let's embrace the blessings we do have. Let's trust that even when things don't go as planned, God is still good, and His presence is our greatest gift.

Today's Challenge:

Take a moment to list five things you're grateful for, even if they seem small. Focus on those blessings throughout the day especially if you're frustrated, or something doesn't go as planned.

1. ____

2. ____

3. ____

4. ____

5. ____

Can you recognize an area in your life where you haven't been as content as you should be? What are some steps you can take to help shift your mindset?

What is the secret that Paul is referring to in Philippians 4:12? Also see Philippians 4:13.

Day 3

Remain Faithful

Therefore, my dear brothers and sisters, stand firm. Let nothing move you.
Always give yourselves fully to the work of the Lord, because you know that your
labor in the Lord is not in vain.
—1 Corinthians 15:58, NIV

Read: Hebrews 11 and Isaiah 9

I'm a big fan of Chip and Joanna, but then again, who isn't, right? Everything they do is jaw-droppingly gorgeous, and somehow, they make it look effortless. Anyone who's gone through a renovation process knows that it's anything but easy. It always looks worse before it gets better, and let's not forget about those unforeseen costs!

Michael and I just finished our basement (technically, he did the work, but since we're one flesh, I'll take a bit of credit too). It looks amazing, but if you had seen it a year ago, you might have doubted it would ever get done. The place was a mess for two years, and the light at the end of the tunnel was dim.

This one-man project was huge. Michael had to design it, frame it, and build it from scratch. And I'm not talking about just one or two rooms. We're talking bedrooms, two storage rooms, a family room, a bathroom—the works!

It was a lot to take on, but if there's one thing I know about Michael, it's this: he doesn't give up. Once he sets his mind to something, there's no turning back, no matter how difficult the journey may be.

Michael's persistence reminds me of what it means to be faithful—not just in projects like this, but in life in general. He's faithful to our marriage, faithful to his word, and most of all, he's faithful to God. He's taught me to push through, even when it doesn't seem like things are coming together. His determination to finish a project mirrors the kind of faithfulness God calls us to live by.

Looking at the book of Genesis, we see faithfulness in action. God promised Abraham that he would be the father of many nations (Genesis 17:4-5), yet Abraham and Sarah waited for years without seeing that promise fulfilled. Even well past the age of having children, they held on to God's promise. Eventually, when Abraham was 100 years old and Sarah was 90, God fulfilled His promise by giving them a son, Isaac (Genesis 21:1-3).

But God's promise didn't end there. It pointed ahead to something far greater—the coming Messiah who would take away the sin of the world. Christmas is a celebration of God's faithfulness to that long-awaited promise, fulfilled through Jesus Christ, His Son. It's a reminder to trust in His unchanging nature and to rest in His unfailing care.

So, just like a renovation project, life can get messy before it gets beautiful. There's dust, uncertainty, and sometimes it feels like we're tearing down more than we're building. But God is faithful, and He's committed to completing the work He's begun in us. Let's remember that, even when we can't see the finished product yet, we can trust the One who's in charge of the project.

"Faithful one, so unchanging, Ageless one, you're my rock of peace.
Lord of all, I depend on you. I call out to you, again and again."
(Brian Doerksen, "Faithful One")

Today's Challenge:

Think about an area in your life where you're waiting for something or trusting God to come through. Ask God to help you trust Him with the process, even when things don't seem to be moving the way you'd hoped. Throughout the day, remind yourself that God is faithful, and that He's working, even when you can't see it.

What connection does Genesis 12:3 and Genesis 22:18 have to Jesus? If you aren't sure, see Galatians 3:16 for help.

How does the story of Abraham and Sarah waiting for Isaac encourage you in your own seasons of waiting?

Be Hopeful

Blessed is the one who trusts in the Lord, whose confidence is in him. They will
be like a tree planted by the water that sends out its roots by
the stream. It does not fear when heat comes; its leaves are always green.
It has no worries in a year of drought and never fails to bear fruit.
—Jeremiah 17:7-8, NIV

Read: Psalm 1 and John 15:1-17

Have you ever heard of a Shepherd's Tree? On the surface, they're not particularly impressive. They tend to be modest and unassuming, with a relatively small trunk compared to other trees. But, as they say, you can't judge a book by its cover. Beneath this ordinary-looking tree lies extraordinary strength. The roots of the Shepherd's Tree reach depths of up to 223 feet, making it the deepest known root structure in the world.

There's a reason this root system is the way it is—it's because of the harsh, dry environment in which it grows. In places like the Kalahari Desert, the tree relies on its deep roots to tap into underground water sources. This allows it to survive in conditions that other plants simply can't. The more I've read about this, the more I've come to love the tenacity of this tree. It doesn't just survive; it does what it takes to thrive.

Jeremiah 17:7-8 tells us, "But blessed is the one who trusts in the Lord, whose confidence is in Him. They will be like a tree planted by the water that sends out its roots by the stream. It does not fear when heat comes; its leaves are always green. It has no worries in a year of drought and never fails to bear fruit."

This passage beautifully captures the idea of being deeply rooted in Christ. Those who trust in the Lord are sustained through difficult times—not because of an outward appearance of faith, but because of what lies beneath. Roots of faith and trust connect us to God, and the more we rely on His strength, the deeper those roots grow.

It's not just Shepherd's Trees that need water—all trees do. Even our Christmas trees need to be standing in water if we want them to last. I'm not talking about the artificial ones you pick up at Target. I'm talking about the real deal—the ones you haul home in the back of your red pickup truck, fresh from the lot. There's something special about a real tree, isn't there? The smell of pine filling your home, bringing back memories of Christmas long ago. But as wonderful as they are, real trees come with a responsibility—they need to be watered. If you don't water your tree, it dries out, the needles get brittle, fall to the floor, and instead of being the colorful, fragrant tree it once was, it becomes lifeless and dull, like most of the plants I've brought home.

Maybe you're facing a challenge this Christmas or having a difficult day. If you're suffering loss or struggling with fear, lower your anchor, my friend, and let His faithfulness hold you firm and secure. More than a wish for better days ahead, hope is there to remind us that God is not done. How do we embrace the Spirit of Hope? The same way the trees do—we soak in His Word to grow stronger in faith. We trust in our God, who is mighty to save. And when the winds of adversity rise up and roar, we stand on His promises—firm and secure.

Today's Challenge:

Spend at least 10 minutes today in prayer or reading Scripture, asking God to help you deepen your trust in Him. Let this be your way of staying connected to the source of true life and peace.

What does it mean to "abide" in Christ (John 15:1-17), and how does this help us bear fruit, even during challenging times?

How does the fruit that we bear, as a healthy tree rooted in Christ, keep us grounded and strong through difficult times?

Day 5

Speak Life

Therefore encourage one another and build each other up, just as in fact you are doing. —1 Thessalonians 5:11, NIV

Read: Ephesians 4

My grandkids come over about once a month and stay for a couple of days. I love every minute of it, but let me just say—they never stop talking. From the moment they walk through the door until they leave, they chit and chat without taking a break. Julia, I can understand perfectly well, but most of the time, Joseph sounds like he's speaking in tongues.

But who am I to talk, right? I'm a woman, and I know how much we love to talk. My friend Sandra and I are a lot like the kids. We have so much to say in so little time that some days we can't fit it all in.

Studies say that, on average, women talk three times as much as men. We speak about 13,000 more words each day. An average man will speak around 7,000 words while his wife speaks 20,000.[1] Of course, this is just an average—some days, I'm sure I speak about five times that much!

Our words are a powerful tool, aren't they? They can build others up, but they can also wound deeply. In James chapter 3, we read about the potential dangers of misusing our tongues. In verse 6, James even says that the tongue "sets the whole course of one's life on fire."

That's a strong but necessary warning when you consider how many lives are damaged by careless words. Marriages are broken, children are wounded, families are divided, and even countries can go to war. The impact of our words can be devastating, and in some cases, those affected never fully heal.

Proverbs 18:21 tells us, "The tongue has the power of life and death, and those who love it will eat its fruit." The tongue can also be used to build up and breathe life into others. Can you think of a better time to do that than now? The holidays give us countless opportunities to share hope with those around us. Whether we're standing in line at the mall or sitting down with friends for a meal, a few words of encouragement can go a long way.

In 1 Thessalonians 5:11, Paul writes, "Therefore encourage one another and build each other up, just as in fact you are doing." This call to encourage one another goes beyond simply "being nice." When we encourage others, we help them overcome adversity and grow stronger in their faith. Christmas is more than just a celebration; it's a proclamation of our faith—an opportunity to share the message of redemption. It's a chance to give the world an answer to our brokenness, a plan to restore what was lost, and rescue us from sin through the gift of Jesus Christ, whose birth brought hope, healing, and new life to all who believe.

[1] *Fiona MacRae, "Sorry to Interrupt Dear, But Women Really Do Talk More Than Men," Mail Online, Science Correspondent.*

Today's Challenge:

Speak life into someone's life today. Whether it's offering an encouraging word to a family member, sending a note to a friend, or sharing a Scripture verse with someone who needs hope, use your words to build others up.

 Can you think of a situation in your life where someone's words had big a big impact on your in either a positive or negative way?

 What are some practical ways you can use your words to bring hope and encouragement to those around you, during the holiday season?

Be Patient

But those who hope in the Lord will renew their strength.
They will soar on wings like eagles; they will run and not grow weary,
they will walk and not be faint. —Isaiah 40:31, NIV

Read: Psalm 37 and Romans 8:18-39

There's something about the Christmas season that brings me back to my youth. The joyful anticipation of waiting is something you never outgrow. Whether we're waiting in line, waiting for guests, or waiting for morning to come, we're reminded that waiting is a part of God's plan. After all, God's people waited thousands of years for the Messiah to come.

My husband and I have different approaches to waiting. He takes his time—he's patient, thoughtful, and makes sure every detail is firmly in place before moving ahead. Me? I'm on the opposite side. I tend to move quickly without pausing to breathe, which isn't always the best choice.

Corrie Ten Boom once said, "When a train goes through a tunnel and it gets dark, you don't throw away the ticket and jump off. You sit still and trust the engineer." That quote gets me every time, because I know I tend to get impatient in times of waiting and uncertainty. God's timing is perfect, and sometimes He asks us to wait—not to delay us, but to develop character through faith, patience, and trust.

When Jesus arrived on that dark, starry night, it wasn't with the grand entrance we might expect. He came quietly, born in a manger, and His timing was part of God's plan. Imagine all that people endured while waiting for Him—centuries of slavery in Egypt, years of wandering in the wilderness, periods of captivity in Babylon, and generations under foreign rulers. Through all of this, God's people clung to the promise of a Messiah, waiting and trusting that, in God's perfect timing, deliverance would come.

The Bible is full of examples of people who waited patiently—Noah waited for rain, Joseph waited in prison, Hannah waited for a child, Abraham waited for the promised son, and the Israelites waited forty years to enter the Promised Land. In each story, God's delay wasn't denial; it was preparation.

If you're in a season of waiting this Christmas—waiting for healing, for employment, for a family, or for another answer to prayer—don't give up. Those who wait on the Lord aren't waiting in vain; you can trust in His wisdom, His timing, and His sovereign power.

So, this Christmas, as you're waiting on God, see it as a season of preparation. Through patience, He's shaping your faith and molding your heart. Trust that when the time comes for His plan to unfold, He will act with wisdom and power.

Let's trust Him together, believing He's never too late, never too early, and always on time.

Today's Challenge:

Identify one area of your life where you're waiting on God. commit to embracing this season of waiting, trusting that His timing is perfect and that He is working for your good, even when you can't yet see the results.

According to Psalm 37, what actions are we encouraged to take while we wait on the Lord? Can you name 6?

Romans 8:18-39 speaks of the hope we have in Christ, even in seasons of waiting. How does focusing on the hope of God's promises help you endure times of uncertainty?

Day 7

Cling to God's Promises

*The Lord gave them rest on every side, just as he had sworn to their ancestors.
Not one of their enemies withstood them; the Lord gave all their enemies into
their hands. Not one of all the Lord's good promises
to Israel failed; every one was fulfilled. —Joshua 21:44-45, NIV*

Read: Numbers 13 & 14:1-11 and Joshua 14

If I could invite anyone over for Christmas, aside from the Savior of course, I'd set a place at my table for Caleb. Over turkey, stuffing, and an extra helping of mashed potatoes, we'd eagerly talk about God. You remember Caleb, don't you? We're introduced to him in Numbers 13. When Moses sent out 12 men to explore the land of Canaan, Caleb was one of them. What I love most about him is that he's tough, tenacious, and he leans on the power of God. He's like a Chuck Norris of faith, considering the giants he conquers as bread for the soul (Numbers 14:9).

Caleb saw what many of us often miss—that the promises of God are unfailing. As my dad used to say, "God said it, I believe it, that settles it." When the Israelites were on the verge of entering the Promised Land, Caleb was one of only two spies who believed they could take it, fully trusting in God's promise despite overwhelming obstacles. Even after 45 years of waiting, Caleb's faith didn't waver. At 85 years old, he was still as bold, strong, and determined as ever, confident that God would fulfill His promises—and He did. Caleb's story is a reminder of what it means to cling to God's Word with unwavering faith, no matter how long it might take.

I've encouraged my readers to incorporate God's promises into their prayers. Not because God needs reminding, but because we do. This practice builds our trust in God and provides comfort and hope, knowing that His promises are sure and steadfast.

I know many of you have suffered great loss, some as recently as this year. I know a lot of you are dealing with sickness, pain, financial burdens, and broken relationships. Even if I don't know you by name, there may be a struggle you're going through too. So I want to encourage you, friend. If you're looking for joy in your sorrow, hope through despair, and peace in the midst of uncertainty, cling to the promises God has given us:

- A promise to never leave you nor forsake you (Deuteronomy 31:6).
- A promise to give strength to the weary and increase the power of the weak (Isaiah 40:29).
- A promise that His grace is sufficient for you (2 Corinthians 12:9).
- A promise that He works all things together for the good of those who love Him (Romans 8:28).
- A promise that those who hope in the Lord will renew their strength (Isaiah 40:31).

Remember, God's promises may not unfold overnight, and sometimes the waiting is hard. But God's timing is perfect, and He's worth waiting for.

Today's Challenge:

Take some time today to either jot down or highlight a few of God's promises that speak to your current situation. Meditate on God's promises throughout the day and pray them back to Him.

Is there a particular promise that you can hold on to (or already do) in your current season of life?

What reasons does the Bible give us that we can trust in the promises of God? Take a look at scriptures like Deuteronomy 7:9, Psalm 33:4, and 2 Timothy 2:13, and consider how they strengthen our trust in Him.

Pursuing
Peace

Day 8

Rest in God's Peace

You will keep in perfect peace those whose minds are steadfast, because they trust in you. —Isaiah 26:3, NIV

Read: Matthew 1&2

When I was a kid, we lived in a couple of homes that were a story and a half. My favorite part? The cubby holes. That's what we called them, anyway. You could get to them through the closet, and most upstairs bedrooms had at least one. It was my space, away from the craziness of everyday life. It was small, but it was quiet, and I loved it. I'd grab a blanket and a little lamp and spend hours tucked away in there, reading comics or playing with my Lite-Brite. I even dragged my Easy-Bake Oven in there a few times, but let's keep that little fire hazard between you and me.

Even now, I still find comfort in small places where I can shut out the noise and distractions of the world.

But do you know what I've come to realize? The sense of peace I felt in that little space is a lot like the comfort I find in God's presence. His peace surrounds me, bringing calm in the midst of a chaotic world.

Isaiah 26:3 tells us, "You will keep in perfect peace those whose minds are steadfast, because they trust in you." Isaiah is reminding us that those who keep their minds focused on God, trusting in Him, will experience true peace.

So, what exactly is peace? The best way I can describe it is as a deep inner calm and a sense of security that comes from trusting in God. (There's also "relational peace," which we'll talk about in the next chapter.)

In this chapter, we're talking about the kind of peace that anchors our hearts and gives us stability in the face of life's storms—the kind of peace that Mary experienced when the angel Gabriel told her that she would bear a child, the Son of God. She must have been overwhelmed and confused, but instead of reacting in fear, she responded in faith, saying, "I am the Lord's servant... May your word to me be fulfilled" (Luke 1:38).

Stop for a minute to think about everything she went through, because we can glean so much from her strength. We've already talked about the uncertainty Mary faced when she learned she would bear the Christ child, and the challenges she faced the night Jesus was born, but the challenges didn't stop there—they continued for years. Matthew 2:13 tells us that the angel of the Lord warned Joseph in a dream that Herod was searching for the child to kill Him. They had to flee to Egypt for safety. Even after Herod died, they were warned again that it wasn't safe to return, so they settled in Nazareth instead.

Can you imagine how chaotic and stressful those first few years must have been? I can't even begin to imagine having someone so bent on killing my child that we'd have to hide just to protect Him. But this was their reality—fleeing, hiding, and constantly on guard.

So, what was Mary's secret? How does a mother like her—or even women like you and me—find peace in the midst of overwhelming and heart-wrenching seasons? We take our eyes off the world and anchor ourselves in the Lord with determined and unwavering trust. And, most importantly, we bring our burdens to Him in prayer.

Today's Challenge:

Write down any fears or anxieties you're carrying and offer them to God in prayer. Throughout the day, remind yourself that Jesus is the Prince of Peace and His peace is available to you. When anxiety creeps in, turn your thoughts back to Him and trust His perfect peace.

According to Philippians 4:6, what two things should we do when we feel anxious?

What are some specific ways that God provides comfort, strength, and rest according to Isaiah 40:29-31?

Peace
on Earth

Be a Peacemaker

Blessed are the peacemakers, for they will be called children of God.
—Matthew 5:9, NIV

Read: Romans 12

When my daughter comes over to spend a weekend with us, especially at this time of year, our favorite thing to do is watch a romantic Hallmark movie and eat chips and dip. She has two children, ages 3 and 5, and their favorite thing to do right now is fight. If it's not one thing, it's another—they argue about toys, about food, and even about who's making the most noise when they're trying to sleep.

I took them to visit my sister Betty the other day. If you've read my blog, you might remember that she's my go-to person for advice on anything from stains to Christmas gifts for that hard-to-buy-for person. If you have a problem, she has a solution.

So, we get to Betty's house, she pulls out some toys for the kids, and sure enough, they both want to play with the same remote-control car. The fighting starts. Instead of dealing with it the way I usually do, Betty pulls out a timer, and they both go silent. Now they're more interested in the timer than in the toy. She shows them how to use it and put 5 minutes on the clock. Bam—problem solved. For the rest of our visit, they took turns, switching between the timer and the car.

With a little creativity and patience, Betty turned a moment of conflict into one of peace. Watching her handle that situation so calmly made me realize something: being a peacemaker doesn't always mean stepping into big, dramatic conflicts. Sometimes, it's as simple as finding a way to bring calm to small, everyday battles.

In this season of Christmas, peace isn't just a word we write on a card—it's a harmony we're called to live by as believers. And if you stop to think about it, we're given countless opportunities. It could be something as simple as calming a tense conversation in a meeting by reminding everyone that we're on the same team, apologizing when we've offended someone, or using kind words to encourage understanding when a friend is frustrated. Instead of taking sides or fueling frustration, we can help mend relationships rather than deepen the divide.

Looking to the Bible, we see that Barnabas played a significant role as a peacemaker. After Paul's conversion, many of the disciples were afraid of him, but Barnabas bridged the gap by vouching for Paul, fostering peace and unity among them (Acts 9:26-27). Likewise, in 1 Samuel 19, Jonathan spoke well of David, hoping to bridge the gap between David and his father, King Saul, who was trying to take David's life.

Sometimes it's easier to stay quiet when there's a divide between people. We don't want to get involved because it feels safer to stay on the sidelines. Stepping in as a peacemaker and saying something kind takes courage, but it might be the first step toward healing and reconciliation. Isn't that what Christmas is truly about? After all, Jesus, the Prince of Peace, prayed for unity even in the Garden of Gethsemane, on the night before He died. Unity was on His heart, and it's the very message of Christmas. As He prayed, "That all of them may be one, Father, just as you are in me and I am in you. May they also be in us so that the world may believe that you have sent me" (John 17:21, NIV).

Today's Challenge:

As you go through your day, look for one opportunity to bring peace into a conversation or situation. Whether it's offering a kind word, encouraging understanding, or simply listening, make an effort to reflect God's peace in your interactions.

What reason does Jesus give for the importance of unity in John 17:20-23? And what do you think He means by this?

According to Matthew 5:23-24, what should we do before approaching God in worship if we have unresolved conflict with someone?

Live With Integrity

A wife of noble character who can find? She is worth far more than
rubies. —*Proverbs 31:10, NIV*

Read: Daniel 3 and 6

We haven't been house hunting in a while, but whenever we have, my
husband and I always seem to look for different things. I'm all about
checking out the bedrooms, eyeing the kitchen layout, and mentally placing
the loveseat and sofa in just the right spot. Meanwhile, my husband heads
straight for the basement, inspecting the beams and foundation. The same
thing happens when we visit friends with new homes—the men go straight
for the foundation while the women ooh and ahh over the kitchen. Don't
get me wrong, as much as I dislike looking at beams and discussing
foundations, I'm thankful he's down there making sure it's well-built. After
all, my kitchen depends on it.

Life is funny that way, isn't it? So many things we enjoy depend on the
unseen. What would a garden be without roots to sustain it? What would
an ocean be like without the currents beneath? If we didn't have the wind
shaping mountains, dunes, and trees over time, we'd be missing the force
that shapes so much beauty around us. It's the unseen things that hold the
most power.

In the same way that a good foundation is of more value than a nice coat
of paint, integrity speaks more about us than talent or charm ever could.
The Bible says, "A wife of noble character who can find? She is worth far
more than rubies" (Proverbs 31:10, NIV). Integrity is about living out that
noble character, not just during the holiday season, but every day. It's the

difference between acting like a Christian and truly being one. We might believe the right things and say the right things, but the real question is, will we do the right thing? Even when no one is watching?

Integrity is the choice to do the right thing when it's difficult, when it goes against the flow, and when we're not expecting praise or approval. It walks in the way of our Savior—a perfect harmony of truth and action. Jesus didn't just speak of love, He embodied it; He didn't just teach humility, He displayed it. He didn't just call for obedience; He was obedient to the point of death—even death on a cross, where His sacrifice spoke louder than words ever could.

Christmas is a time of giving and sharing, opening the door to opportunities that reflect the sacrificial love of our Lord. The way we choose to live out our faith speaks volumes about the God we serve.

So, what does integrity look like this holiday season? Perhaps it's choosing a kind word instead of engaging in gossip. Maybe it's resisting the urge to snap at the overwhelmed cashier. It might be showing patience when family gatherings get stressful. It could mean honoring a commitment when something more exciting comes up. And it might be giving to someone in secret without expecting thanks in return.

Today's Challenge:

Today, look for an opportunity to choose integrity over convenience. Whether it's staying true to your word, offering kindness in a tough situation, or doing something good without seeking recognition, let your actions align with your faith. Ask yourself, "What does it look like to honor God through my choices today, even when no one is watching?"

What qualities are demonstrated alongside integrity in the story of Daniel's friends in Daniel chapter 3?

What qualities are demonstrated alongside integrity in the story of Daniel in Daniel chapter 6?

Practice Selflessness

Do nothing out of selfish ambition or vain conceit. Rather, in humility value others above yourselves, not looking to your own interests but each of you to the interests of the others. —Philippians 2:3-4, NIV

Read: Isaiah 53

It's beginning to look a lot like Christmas. Everywhere you go, there's a focus on what you'll get, if you haven't bought it yet, with credit cards and shopping bags in tow. Sounds a little self-centered, doesn't it? But here's the thing: the most wonderful time of the year can easily turn into the most selfish time of the year if we're not careful. If we don't step back and realign our hearts, Christmas can become all about what we can get instead of what we're called to give.

We live in a world that's obsessed with self. Everywhere you turn, people want to be seen, heard, and known. Articles and headlines flood us with words like self-esteem, self-worth, self-confidence, self-help... the list goes on. All of these things push us to put ourselves at the center of our lives, and if we're not intentional, we can lose focus of what's really important.

So where does Christmas fit into all of this? It doesn't. Christmas isn't meant to squeeze alongside a self-centered life. It's meant to replace it. The Bible tells us to put off our old self—our self-centered ways—and to be made new in the attitude of our minds. We're called to put on a new self, created to be like God in true righteousness and holiness (Ephesians 4:22-24).

Christmas is the perfect reminder of that transformation. The gift we celebrate isn't wrapped in paper or tied with a bow—it's the gift of a Savior who left the glory of heaven to walk among us. Jesus didn't come for His own gain; He came for ours. He humbled Himself to take on human form (Philippians 2:6-7), living with the struggles and pains we face, and ultimately giving His life for our salvation. His birth was just the beginning of His incredible journey to the cross—the ultimate act of selflessness. Isaiah 53:5 tells us, "But he was pierced for our transgressions, he was crushed for our iniquities; the punishment that brought us peace was on him, and by his wounds we are healed." His suffering and sacrifice were for our redemption, not His own benefit.

So, let's ask ourselves: How can we live that out?

Christmas isn't about what we'll get; it's about what we're called to give. It's not about who's going to serve us, but how we can serve others. What does it look like to embrace the spirit of Christmas? It's focusing on how we can give—without expecting anything in return. It's sharing Christmas dinner with someone who's alone. It's baking shortbread cookies for someone who's sick. It's offering a gift to someone in need. It's serving behind the scenes without recognition. It's showing grace to a family member who tests your patience.

Christmas isn't measured by the presents we give or receive, but by the selfless way we love and serve others. Jesus came to serve, not to be served, and He invites us to do the same. And so, this Christmas, let's take off the old and put on the new. Let's embrace selfless love by living it out.

Today's Challenge:

Choose one selfless act today that reflects the true spirit of Christmas. Whether it's calling someone who's lonely, offering a meal to someone in need, or simply showing extra patience and kindness to a family member.

What are three specific ways Jesus showed selflessness throughout His life and ministry?

What are some selfless acts you've seen from others over the years? And how, if at all, has that inspired the way you celebrate Christmas?

Create Peace Within

Finally, brothers and sisters, whatever is true, whatever is noble, whatever is right, whatever is pure, whatever is lovely, whatever is admirable—if anything is excellent or praiseworthy—think about such things.
—Philippians 4:8, NIV

Read: Philippians 4

Have you ever found yourself stuck in a cycle of negative thinking? Maybe it happens at Christmas. When you're pulled in a hundred different directions—when the to-do lists are long, the schedule's full, and it feels like there's no time left for a silent night. All kinds of emotions come up when we take on too much. Worry, frustration, and stress can easily rob us of peace, which is why it's important to open our Bibles and take in Paul's words:

"Finally, brothers and sisters, whatever is true, whatever is noble, whatever is right, whatever is pure, whatever is lovely, whatever is admirable—if anything is excellent or praiseworthy—think about such things." (Philippians 4:8, NIV)

Those are beautiful words, but let's be honest—how often do we take them to heart? If you're anything like me, you have days when your glass is half empty. Negative thoughts sneak in and overshadow your day. You find yourself worried, frustrated, and tense.

So, how do we shift our thoughts? How do we go from stinkin' thinkin' to the kind of mindset Paul is talking about? How do we reclaim the peace we long for at Christmas?

Paul gives us the answer in the very next verse: "Whatever you have learned or received or heard from me, or seen in me—put it into practice. And the God of peace will be with you." (Philippians 4:9, NIV)

Notice the word "practice." Paul emphasizes that this kind of thinking isn't something we accomplish in one day; it's something we practice day after day. Of course, we'll have days when life throws us off track and negative thoughts find their way back. We're not expected to be perfect, but we should be progressing, and that's possible when we take God's Word to heart and put His truth into practice. We do this by being intentional about what we're feeding our minds and where we allow them to dwell.

The best thing about this is that the way we think changes the way we live. Paul is telling us that practicing a right way of thinking brings peace. He's not saying that peace comes after the hustle and bustle of the season is over; he's pointing out the fact that peace comes from aligning our lives with God's truth.

Finally, you can't expect a garden to grow if you just water bare ground. The first step is planting a seed. You have to get in there, dig up the soil, and place that seed with intention. We do that by learning and receiving God's Word. That's where our thoughts are transformed—planting truth in our hearts and allowing His peace to take root.

Today's Challenge:

When you feel negativity creeping in, take a moment to pause and reflect on Philippians 4:8. Write down three things that are true, noble, or praiseworthy that you can focus on instead. If you catch yourself dwelling on frustrations or worries, redirect your thoughts to these positive truths and remind yourself of God's promises.

What are some examples of 'true, noble, and admirable' thoughts you can focus on in times of stress or frustration? How can these thoughts shift your mindset during difficult seasons?

What four actions does Paul encourage us to take in Philippians 4:9? And how can we apply them to our lives today?

Embrace Humility

And being found in appearance as a man, he humbled himself by becoming obedient to death—even death on a cross! —Philippians 2:8, NIV

Read: Luke 7:36-50 and Philippians 2:1-11

Yesterday, I took an afternoon nap, but instead of playing my usual ambient sounds, I decided to listen to traffic. The sound of tires squealing, horns honking, and the whir of motors in the distance brought me back to our home on the corner when life was simple and carefree. Little did my parents know at the time that one of my favorite things to do back then was to climb the billboard, settle into my place on the ledge, and take in the view of the traffic below.

There's something about high places that fascinates me. And while I love the view from a billboard, nothing compares to the top of a mountain. There's a feeling of awe and wonder when you take in the view of the valley below. It's amazing how some of the lowest places on earth hold the greatest beauty, isn't it? So it is with mankind. The Bible tells us, "It is better to be lowly in spirit among the humble than to divide the spoil with the proud." (Proverbs 16:19 NIV)

The word "humble" comes from the Latin word *humilis*, which literally means "low" or "grounded." It emphasizes the idea of being close to the earth or low in status in much the same way that kneeling does.

In Luke chapter 7, we find Jesus at the home of Simon the Pharisee. We also find a "sinful" woman, most likely a prostitute, who was there with an alabaster jar of perfume. Though she was sinful, we see this woman washing Christ's feet with her tears and wiping them with her hair. Then, sparing no expense, she poured the costly perfume on His feet.

In biblical times, it was common practice for servants to wash the feet of guests. This tradition had both practical and symbolic significance, as foot washing was considered an act of hospitality, humility, and care. Since people typically wore sandals while walking on dusty, dirty roads, their feet would naturally become dirty after traveling, especially over long distances. Washing a guest's feet upon arrival was a way to refresh them and make them comfortable. If there was no servant in the home, the host would furnish a basin of water for the guest to wash their own feet. (International Standard Bible Encyclopedia) During this visit, Simon neglected to serve Him. His lack of humility was a stark contrast to the woman who was ready and willing to wash Jesus' feet with her tears and dry them with the hair on her head.

As we celebrate Christmas this year, let's remember that the Spirit of Christmas is found in the way we humbly love and serve others. It's helping with dishes after a meal, it's cooking a meal for someone in need, it's shoveling a driveway without being asked, and it's offering support without seeking recognition. The Spirit of Christmas is found in the whisper of love that reflects the humble Spirit of God. Embrace the humble Spirit of Christ this year by reflecting the light of His love.

Today's Challenge:

Find a quiet way to practice humility by putting someone else's needs ahead of your own. Whether it's letting someone go ahead of you in line, doing a task at home or work that usually gets overlooked, or offering a sincere apology when it's difficult, choose an action that requires you to step back and allow others to be first.

Who was the humblest man in the Bible, next to Jesus? And, what does the word "humble" mean when used to describe someone?

After Jesus washed the disciples' feet, He said, "I have set you an example that you should do as I have done for you." How can we live out this commandment?

Day 14

Reflect Christ's Character

He was oppressed and afflicted, yet he did not open his mouth; he was led like a lamb to the slaughter, and as a sheep before its shearers is silent, so he did not open his mouth —Isaiah 53:7, NIV

Read: Luke 23

One of the first jobs I ever had was working as a cashier at Kmart. Sporting their teal-colored jacket, I made sure to say, "Thank you for shopping our Kmart," at the end of every transaction.

After three years, I was great at my job. I knew all the codes and most of the customers. I could ring people through quickly, but even then, we had the odd price check that would slow the line down. Most people were okay with a five-minute delay—others, not so much. And Christmas? That was a whole different ball of wax. I worked there during the Cabbage Patch craze. Imagine people bursting through the doors, running, crying, yelling, and shoving each other to get their hands on a doll. Picture the toilet paper shortage of 2020 and you'll get an idea of what it was like. Parents and grandparents would line up for hours if they heard a shipment arrived. And if they went home empty-handed, they weren't too happy with us. I enjoyed working there, but Christmas was off the wall at times. One year I had a customer sit on the floor in protest because the price check was taking too long.

I learned that difficult people will always be a part of our lives. As soon as one leaves, the next one is right there in line. But here's the thing: difficult people don't have the power to determine the tone of our day—unless we let them. They don't dictate our attitude or control our response. What they do is offer us a divine opportunity to walk in Christ-likeness, to reflect the character of our Savior.

For many, getting together with family during the holiday season is a peaceful and joyful time. But for others, it feels more like a thorn in the flesh. You're expected to go here and there, but deep down, you know it's going to be tough. We all want that Norman Rockwell Christmas—everyone smiling while Dad carves the turkey—but sometimes God gives us a challenge. Sometimes we find ourselves sitting at the table with people who know just how to push our buttons. They question your choices, your faith, maybe even the way you raise your children. Some folks seem to have a knack for making you feel small with just a few words.

But as followers of Christ, we're called to a higher standard. We don't respond like the world does. Instead, we're invited to reflect the patience and longsuffering of Jesus. When He was mocked, He didn't retaliate. When He was challenged, He didn't strike back. He could have fought, could have said more, done more, but He chose silence and surrender. Why? So that even those who stood against Him might be saved.

Sisters, may we be like the lamb—silent, still, and obedient in the hands of our Master. When the pressure builds, when comfort is stripped away, may we bear it well, trusting that God is at work even when things are hard. Jesus faced more pain and hostility than we will ever know, yet He remained steadfast in His love and patience.

Today's Challenge:

If you encounter a difficult person, take a deep breath and remind yourself that you have the power to choose your response. Choose wisely by following Christ's example of humility, patience and grace.

According to Colossians 3:12-13, how does Paul instruct believers to deal with difficult people? What specific attributes does he mention in that verse?

How can praying for those who mistreat us change our perspective and attitude toward them?

Spreading
Joy

Spread Joy

May the God of hope fill you with all joy and peace as you trust in him, so that you may overflow with hope by the power of the Holy Spirit.
—Romans 15:13, NIV

Read: Philippians 1

My daughter's family moved four hours north, where they've settled into a beautiful home with a yard big enough for Maddy and the kids to raise a few chickens. But let me tell you, what I love most about their new place is the Northern Lights. The farther north you live, the more breathtaking and frequent they are. Just the other day, they posted a photo of the most stunning streaks of green and red, blending together across the sky with an almost surreal glow. I could hardly believe it was real.

That image got me thinking about something else today—the night of Christ's birth. Picture the shepherds, out in the field, going about their ordinary, everyday tasks when the angel of the Lord appeared, and the glory of God lit up the night around them. But as incredible as that sight must have been, it's the words the angel spoke that really get me. "Do not be afraid. I bring you good news that will cause great joy for all the people. Today in the town of David a Savior has been born to you; he is the Messiah, the Lord."

Joy. Real, soul-deep joy. You see, joy is a theme that weaves itself throughout the gospel of Christ—from the night of His birth to the early days of the church, as the apostles took this good news to the world. And let me tell you, one of the clearest places you see this joy in the Bible is in the book of Philippians. What's remarkable about Philippians is that Paul wrote this letter while he was under house arrest in Rome. He could have easily complained, but instead, he chose joy and used his circumstances to advance the gospel. His attitude didn't just encourage the Philippian church back then—it has continued to strengthen and inspire countless believers, including us, to this very day. Paul's example shows us that joy isn't just a feeling we have when life is easy; it's something we can choose in every circumstance.

The message of joy isn't something to be separated from Christmas; it's deeply embedded in what Christmas is all about. But here's the thing: that joy isn't meant to stay locked away. Just like Paul, we are called to spread joy wherever we are, no matter what challenges we face. Paul didn't wait for his situation to improve before he shared the good news—he shared it right in the middle of his struggles. And when we do the same—when we spread joy in the midst of our own hardships—we offer hope to a world that's desperately in need of it.

Romans 15:13 says, "May the God of hope fill you with all joy and peace as you trust in him, so that you may overflow with hope by the power of the Holy Spirit." Do you see that? This verse shows us that when we trust in God, He fills us with joy and peace, and that joy and peace overflow. It spills out onto the people around us. When we live with the joy that comes from knowing Christ, we don't just keep it to ourselves—our joy, like Paul's, can inspire others to seek Christ, no matter where they are in life. So let's be intentional about choosing joy and sharing it, for the glory of God and for the encouragement of those around us.

Today's Challenge:

Choose to spread joy in a small but meaningful way. It could be through a kind word, a note of encouragement, or a thoughtful gesture to someone who might need a little extra joy. Ask God to show you how you can be a light to someone today.

How can Paul's example in Philippians chapter 1 encourage us to share the gospel and spread joy in our own circumstances?

What reason do we find in James 1:2-4 to have joy in the midst of our trials?

Be Joyful in Giving

In everything I did, I showed you that by this kind of hard work we must help the weak, remembering the words the Lord Jesus himself said: "It is more blessed to give than to receive." —Acts 20:35, NIV

Read: Luke 19:1-9 and 2 Corinthians 9

Emma was a new Christian, eager to grow in her faith, but struggling to find joy during the Christmas season. One afternoon, as she and her neighbor, Miss Maggie—a feisty, spirit-filled woman—sat together for their usual Bible study and tea, Emma poured out her heart. "I just don't feel like I belong. I don't have a ministry, and I don't feel useful," she confessed.

Miss Maggie, never one to waste words, smiled warmly. "Emma, I want you to come someplace with me tomorrow night. Be ready at 5."

Curious but trusting her neighbor, Emma agreed. The next evening, Miss Maggie pulled up in her old station wagon, and they drove across town to a local shelter. When they arrived, Emma was surprised to see volunteers busy preparing dinner for the homeless. Miss Maggie handed her an apron with a wink. "Sometimes, the best way to find joy is to give it away."

Emma joined in, serving meals and talking with people who were down on their luck. One elderly man caught her attention. He looked lonely, and without a second thought, she brought him a plate and sat with him for a while, listening to his story. In that moment, she realized that her own troubles seemed so much smaller compared to the needs around her.

As they drove home later that night, Miss Maggie looked over at Emma with a knowing smile. "How do you feel now, dear?"

Emma thought for a moment. "I feel...lighter," she said, surprised at the peace in her heart.

"That's the joy of giving, sweet girl," Miss Maggie replied. "When we take our eyes off ourselves and focus on others, we discover the kind of joy that comes from the Lord."

We see a beautiful example of this in the story of Zacchaeus. When Jesus called Zacchaeus down from the tree and invited Himself to his home, Zacchaeus experienced a transformation. His natural response to the grace and love of Jesus was to give—he joyfully pledged to give half of his possessions to the poor and repay anyone he had wronged four times over (Luke 19:8). His generosity flowed out of the joy he found in Christ, showing us that true joy comes from giving in response to God's love.

It's easy to get caught up in our own worries and the busyness of life, especially at Christmas, but the joy of giving is where we find true fulfillment. Whether it's through offering a meal, lending a hand, or simply being present with someone who needs encouragement, we reflect the love of Christ in every act of kindness. As Acts 20:35 reminds us, "It is more blessed to give than to receive."

So, as we celebrate the greatest gift of all—Jesus Christ—let's remember that we're never more like Him than when we are giving of ourselves. The joy of Christmas is found not in what we receive, but in how we share His love with those around us.

Today's Challenge:

Give a thoughtful gift to someone in your life. It doesn't have to be something bought from a store—it could be homemade, like baking, a handwritten letter, or even a small piece of art. The important part is that the gift reflects your care and thought for that person.

Read 2 Corinthians 9:6-7. What does Paul say about the attitude we should have when giving, and how might this perspective change how we approach helping others, especially during the Christmas season?

How can giving generously—whether time, resources, or kindness—transform our own hearts as we reflect Christ's love to others?

Day 17

Celebrate God's Goodness

For the Lord is good and his love endures forever;
his faithfulness continues through all generations.
—Psalm 100:5, NIV

Read: Luke 5:1-11 and John 6:1-14

Have you ever had a moment where you realized just how good God has been to you? I mean, one of those moments where His blessings come pouring in, overflowing your "nets" in ways you couldn't even imagine? That's exactly what happened to Simon Peter in Luke 5. Here was a man who'd been fishing all night—no luck, nothing to show for all his hard work. Then, Jesus steps in with a simple instruction: "Put out into deep water, and let down the nets for a catch" (Luke 5:4). Now, I don't know about you, but I might have been tempted to question that. After all, Simon was the expert fisherman, not Jesus. Yet Simon obeyed, and what happened next? His nets weren't just full; they were full to the point of breaking! That's the kind of blessing God brings—overflowing, abundant, more than we ever dare to expect.

But here's the part that really moves me: Simon wasn't just dazzled by the miracle—he dropped to his knees in humility, overcome by the presence of Jesus Himself. He knew that this incredible blessing wasn't just about the fish; it was about the Giver, the One who knew exactly what he needed and met him right there in that moment. And that brings me to this thought— how many times have my own "nets" been full to breaking, yet I've been too distracted by the blessing to remember the One who gave it to me?

Christmas is a season full of blessings and beautiful moments, isn't it? Family gatherings, warm meals, lights, and gifts—they're all around us. But just like Simon, we have the chance to pause, to look past the gifts and focus on the Giver. Every one of these blessings is a reminder of the goodness of God, who loves us and delights in us. And as wonderful as each gift is, they are really just a glimpse of His heart—ways for us to remember that Jesus Himself is the greatest gift of all.

So this Christmas, let's make a conscious choice. Instead of letting the gifts, the busyness, and even the joyful chaos distract us, let's remember who it all points to. Let's celebrate not just what He's given, but who He is. He's our Provider, our Savior, our ever-present Help. And every single time He fills our nets, He's inviting us to come closer, to know Him more, and to share His joy.

Friend, there's something life-changing about taking the time to celebrate God's goodness—to let each blessing turn your heart back to Him. Let's come to the feet of Jesus, just like Simon did, with hearts that are grateful and eyes that see beyond the gifts. This season, may we be filled with joy—not because our nets are full, but because we know the One who fills them. After all, the best part of the blessings is knowing the One who gives them, who loves us more than we could ever imagine. And in that knowledge, there's a deep, abiding peace that nothing else can offer.

Today's Challenge:

Thank God for three simple blessings you might normally overlook—a warm meal, a kind word, or a moment of peace. Write them down and offer a quick prayer of thanks, letting His goodness bring joy to your day.

The goodness of God is shown in many ways—from being our Savior to our Provider. Connect a verse from the Bible to each of the following words that point to the goodness of God.

- Helper -

- Savior -

- Provider -

- Comforter -

- Redeemer -

- Healer -

Live in Gratitude

Give thanks in all circumstances; for this is God's will for you
in Christ Jesus. —1 Thessalonians 5:18, NIV

Read: Luke 17:11-19 and Psalm 100

The year that Madison was born, Michael was on his own for Brendan's birthday. It was a week before Christmas, and I had just gotten home from the hospital, recuperating from a C-section. I decided to stay back and wrap some gifts while taking care of the baby. Thankfully, Michael and his brother offered to host the party—eight energetic kids on the loose, full of sugar, at a local arcade.

Apparently, after buying them lunch, giving them cake, and supplying them with handfuls of tokens, Michael had a run-in with a six-year-old girl. With her hands on her hips and shoulders pulled back, she announced, "I demand more tokens!"

"It's ungrateful, but not all that out of the ordinary for kids," I told Michael that evening. The more I thought about it, the more I realized that ungratefulness isn't all that out of the ordinary for adults either. For many people, Christmas becomes a season of "give and give me some more." Stores are overrun on Boxing Day, and it's not just because people are exchanging their gifts—they're filling their carts with everything they wanted but didn't get the day before.

In many ways, it mirrors our prayer life. James 4:3 says, "When you ask, you do not receive, because you ask with wrong motives, that you may spend what you get on your pleasures." We're often willing to pray, but do we treat our prayers like a wish list? And as the days unfold, are we truly ready to give thanks for all things? Sure, we may thank God for the big blessings, but do we thank Him for the ordinary ones we've come to expect? Do we thank Him in the midst of our trials? Do we thank Him when life doesn't go as we planned?

Billy Graham once said, "A spirit of thankfulness is one of the most distinctive marks of a Christian whose heart is attuned to the Lord."

This brings to mind the story of the ten lepers in Luke 17. These men, afflicted and cast out, found themselves on the fringes of society. When they saw Jesus, they recognized Him as their only hope, crying out, "Master, have pity on us!" Jesus, in His mercy, instructed them to go and show themselves to the priests, and as they went, all ten were miraculously healed. But only one—a Samaritan, an outsider among outsiders—turned back to give thanks.

Jesus noticed his return and asked, "Were not all ten cleansed? Where are the other nine?" It's a question that echoes for us today. Are we among the nine who quickly receive but rarely return to give thanks to God? Or do we choose the path of the one grateful leper, who recognized that his healing came from a hand far greater than his own?

There's a difference between being healed and being whole. All ten lepers received physical healing, but only one experienced the deeper wholeness that comes through faith and gratitude. The Samaritan leper's heart was transformed because he chose to acknowledge and give thanks to God, seeing beyond the gift to the Giver.

As we approach Christmas, let's step back from the "give me" mentality that so easily surrounds us. Let's cultivate a spirit of thankfulness—a heart willing to return to God, no matter what we receive or how our prayers are answered.

Today's Challenge:

Take a few minutes today to list five things you're grateful for, no matter how small they might seem. Then, spend a moment in prayer, giving thanks for each one. Let this be a reminder of God's constant presence and goodness, even in the ordinary moments.

In Luke 17:11-19, what distinguishes the one leper who returned to Jesus from the other nine? What can this teach us about the importance of gratitude in our own lives?

What are some specific ways that Psalm 100 encourages us to express gratitude to God?

Joyfully Serve

Let us not become weary in doing good, for at the proper time we will reap a harvest if we do not give up. —Galatians 6:9, NIV

Read: Proverbs 31:10-31

One of my all-time favorite memories was captured in a photo of my son Nathaniel, back when he was about eight years old. I had stepped away from rolling dough for a moment, and when I came back, there he was—on his hands and knees, leaning over the cupboard, rolling dough with such concentration. Caught in the act, knee-deep in baking, he had this quiet joy on his face, as if he was doing exactly what he was meant to do.

That's classic Nathaniel. He's 23 now, and his heart for serving others has only grown. He holds doors open, carries groceries, fills water glasses without being asked, and even pulls weeds from the garden. It's more than just kindness; it's a willingness to do good, the kind of "well-doing" that Paul talks about in Galatians.

Paul writes, "Let us not become weary in doing good, for at the proper time we will reap a harvest if we do not give up. Therefore, as we have opportunity, let us do good to all people, especially to those who belong to the family of believers." (Galatians 6:9-10, NIV).

This isn't just about being a "good" person; it's about deep, intentional goodness—the kind that gives without expecting anything in return. It's a light that shines simply because that's what light does. As Matthew Henry said, "Our present time is seed time; in the other world, we shall reap as we sow now."

Isn't that what this season is about? Christmas invites us to sow seeds of joy, to give from a place of love, expecting nothing in return. But, if we're honest, it can be easy to grow weary, can't it? We pour ourselves into gift-giving, meal-prepping, and serving our families, and sometimes, we wonder if anyone even notices. Yet, Paul reminds us not to lose heart. The joy in serving doesn't come from applause or recognition; it comes from knowing we're reflecting the love and kindness of Christ.

Do you remember that little song, "This Little Light of Mine?" We sang it as kids, putting our fingers up like little candles, promising not to hide our light. But what is that light, really? It's more than just a declaration of faith; it's a way of life. It's letting the goodness of God show up in the small, everyday moments—like rolling dough beside your mom or offering a helping hand to someone in need.

Jesus said, "Let your light shine before others, that they may see your good deeds and glorify your Father in heaven" (Matthew 5:16). This Christmas, let's let our light shine through acts of joyful service. Let's make it a season of spreading joy—not just with decorations or presents, but with the kind of goodness that comes from a grateful heart. When we serve joyfully, we reflect the love and kindness of Christ, and that's a gift that lasts well beyond the season.

So, as you move through the busy days ahead, remember that every small act of kindness is a seed. And even if we don't see the fruit right away, we can trust that God will use those seeds in ways we may never know. Let's joyfully serve, let our light shine, and celebrate the goodness of God with every step.

Today's Challenge:

Look for one simple way to serve someone today without expecting anything in return. Maybe it's holding the door for a stranger, refilling someone's coffee, or lending a listening ear. As you do this, take a moment to silently thank God for the opportunity to reflect His goodness. Let it be a reminder of how even the smallest acts can spread joy.

Read Proverbs 31:10-31. What are some specific qualities of the 'woman of noble character,' that reflect a heart for serving others?

Proverbs 31:20 says, "She opens her arms to the poor and extends her hands to the needy." What are some practical ways we can follow her example during the holiday season?

Share the Good News

For Christ did not send me to baptize, but to preach the gospel—not with wisdom and eloquence, lest the cross of Christ be emptied of its power.
—1 Corinthians 1:17 (NIV)

Read: 1 Corinthians 2

One Sunday morning, my mom and dad were sitting in church, listening closely as the pastor spoke about the power of sharing the gospel. He painted a picture of the gospel as a seed, explaining how even a single one, when planted, grows and produces more seeds over time. "If you keep planting those seeds," he said, "they'll multiply again and again."

To help everyone remember that message, the pastor asked the ushers to pass out two seeds to each person in the congregation. It was a simple but powerful reminder, as if he were saying, "Plant the good news and watch it grow."

The following summer, after another Sunday service, my dad walked up to the pastor and handed him a small paper bag. Surprised, the pastor asked, "What is this?"

My dad smiled and replied, "These are the seeds you gave us last year. I planted them, and I wanted to show you how they multiplied." Each seed was a reminder of how the gospel spreads, reaching further than we might ever see.

A few years later, after my dad passed away, we gathered by his graveside to say our goodbyes. During that tender moment, the pastor reached into his pocket and pulled out that same small bag. Holding it up, he said, "I got this bag of seeds from your father a couple of years ago. These seeds represent the gospel he planted in each one of your lives." Then, as he reached into the bag to pass out the seeds, he continued, "And now, it's your turn to keep planting those seeds."

If there was one thing about my dad, it's that he loved sharing the gospel. He saw it the same way the angels did the night they appeared to the shepherds—as good tidings of great joy. The coming of Christ was good news that had to be shared. And do you know who else shared the gospel? The shepherds. Despite their low social status, God chose them to be among the first people to hear and spread the news of Jesus' birth. The Bible tells us that after they went to Bethlehem to see the child, they "spread the word concerning what had been told them about this child" (Luke 2:17). The choice of these humble, marginalized men to announce the arrival of Jesus reveals an important theme in the gospel: God often works through the least likely people to carry out His plans.

And you know what? Sharing the gospel doesn't have to be a 45-minute sermon. It doesn't require a well-known speaker or someone with thousands of followers. God can use each of us right where we are—whether we're influential or unnoticed—to share His love and truth. Often, the most meaningful ways we share the gospel are through small acts of kindness, a listening ear, or a simple word of encouragement. It's those small, sincere moments that touch hearts the most.

Today's Challenge:

Share something meaningful about your faith with someone today. It doesn't have to be lengthy and in fact can be simple—follow God's lead. Let your words reflect the purity and power of the gospel message, trusting that God will work through even the humblest efforts.

According to 1 Corinthians 2:4-5, what did Paul rely on instead of wise and persuasive words? And why was that important?

According to 1 Corinthians 1:26, what three characteristics does Paul say were *not* typical among those called by God? How can this encourage us when we feel inadequate in sharing the gospel? (also see 1 Corinthians 1:27)

Day 21

Seek God's Presence Daily

The Word became flesh and made his dwelling among us. We have seen his glory, the glory of the one and only Son, who came from the Father, full of grace and truth. —John 1:14, NIV

Read: John 1

Last Christmas, there was a knock on our door. When I opened it, three people stood on our front steps, bundled up with rosy cheeks and wide smiles. One held a guitar, another shook sleigh bells, and they began singing Christmas carols right there on our doorstep. Their voices floated through the cold air, filling our home with warmth. Just listening to them sing brought me back to all those years when caroling was something we did every December, moving from house to house, sharing joy with neighbors. I knew the words to so many carols back then.

To be honest, I never stopped to think about what the words really meant, but this time was different. The words hit me in a new way, and I stood there, truly listening. One line from "Hark! The Herald Angels Sing" stood out: "Pleased as man with man to dwell, Jesus, our Immanuel."

Take a moment and let that sink in. Did you know it has always been God's desire to dwell with His people? Not just to watch over us from a distance, but to be with us, right here in our lives.

The name Immanuel—"God with us"—captures this perfectly. God didn't just send a messenger or an angel; He came Himself, stepping into our world as Jesus, living among us, and sharing in our joys and struggles.

He didn't come with palace grandeur or worldly power. Instead, He chose to come humbly, stepping into our broken world to bring hope.

The words of that carol echo the prophecy in Isaiah: "The virgin will conceive and give birth to a son, and they will call him Immanuel" (Matthew 1:23). God had been promising this for centuries—a Savior who would make His home with us.

Throughout the Bible, we see God's heart for dwelling with His people. In the Old Testament, God's presence was with the Israelites in the form of a cloud by day and fire by night. Later, He instructed them to build a tabernacle, a special place where He could be near them. But even then, there was a sense of separation. Only the high priest could enter the Holy of Holies, and even that was only once a year. God's desire wasn't to keep us at a distance. He wanted intimacy with His people—a closeness that would break down every barrier.

And that's what He did through Jesus. John 1:14 tells us, "The Word became flesh and made his dwelling among us." Jesus took on human form, not just for a moment, but to fully live as one of us, experiencing our pain, our joy, and our temptations. He was "pleased as man with man to dwell." God didn't come reluctantly; He came joyfully, choosing to make His home with us, knowing it would cost Him everything.

This is the heart of the gospel—that God's love compelled Him to draw near, to bridge the gap, to make a way for us to know Him personally. And as we reflect on these carols this season, don't just sing the words; let the message sink in. God's desire is still the same today. He wants to dwell with us, right here, right now, bringing us hope, comfort, and peace. That's Immanuel. That's the miracle of Christmas.

Today's Challenge:

As you go about your day today—whether you're working, cooking, or running errands—play some Christmas carols and really listen to the words. Let them sink in. Reflect on the message of each song and allow the reminder of God's love and presence to fill your heart with hope and peace.

Read John 1:14. What does it mean for 'the Word' to become flesh and make His dwelling among us?

We know that God desires to be close to us. What are some ways that you intentionally draw closer to Him?

Reflecting Love

Terri's Trinkets
and Toys

Love Unconditionally

We love because he first loved us. —1 John 4:19, NIV

Read: Luke 2:1-20 and Matthew 5:43-48

What makes the spirit of Christmas so wonderful? I've seen it in the twinkling lights, the greeting cards, and gifts under the tree. I've tasted it in sugar cookies, candy canes, and hot chocolate by the fire. I've smelled it in the scent of warm cinnamon and my mom's traditional stuffing. I've felt it in the presence of family and friends, and I've heard it in the jingle of bells and the melody of carolers at my door. Yes, the spirit of Christmas can be found all around us, but the true heartbeat of this season comes from something far greater. It flows from a vessel of love wrapped in swaddling clothes and lying in a manger—Jesus Christ. His love and gift of grace are what make this season truly meaningful. It's about the Savior who came to be with us, offering hope, peace, and the promise of eternal life.

The Bible tells us, "But God demonstrates his own love for us in this: While we were still sinners, Christ died for us" (Romans 5:8). Isn't that amazing? Dying for the sinner? I can imagine giving my life for my husband or children, but for someone who hurt me or turned their back on me? That's a love so deep and sacrificial, it's beyond comprehension. Yet, that's what Jesus did. He didn't wait for us to earn His love. He reached out to us at our lowest, offering grace when we least deserved it.

The other day, I was having coffee with a friend, and she shared some struggles she was facing with a relative. Because of the hurtful behavior, she had decided to cut ties. "Do you think I made the right decision?" she asked.

It wasn't my place to make that call, but I offered a few thoughts from a Christian perspective.

First, I reminded her that there are times we need boundaries to protect ourselves and our loved ones, especially our children. We can be kind while still keeping a healthy distance. Sometimes, stepping back is necessary.

Then I reminded her of something else: it's easy to love those who love us back. The real challenge is loving those who are difficult to love—the ones who have hurt us. That's where we reflect the heart of Christ, who walked in sacrificial love. True love isn't about what we get in return. It's rooted in the love God has already shown us, a love that seeks no reward. As James 1:17 says, "Every good and perfect gift is from above, coming down from the Father."

The reason Jesus came wasn't for applause or recognition—it was love, pure and simple. He clothed Himself in humanity and was born in one of the humblest places—a stable. Not an ideal birthplace for anyone, let alone a king. But it was deliberate. Jesus came humbly to meet us exactly where we are.

This Christmas, as we enjoy all the special moments, let's remember where the real spirit of the season begins—with a Savior who came to be with us, to love us fully, even when we didn't deserve it. That's what makes this season truly wonderful.

Today's Challenge:

Find one person in your life today who might be difficult to love or someone you may have distanced yourself from. Reach out to them in a kind way, whether it's with a simple text, a prayer, or a thoughtful gesture. This small act of grace reflects the spirit of Christ's sacrificial love—loving others because He first loved us. Remember, it's easy to love those who love us, but the real challenge lies in loving those who are harder to love.

What does Matthew 5:43-48 teach us about the way we should respond to those who have hurt us?

What kind of love does God call us to show others, according to this passage? How can you apply this in your relationships?

Forgive Freely

*Bear with each other and forgive one another if any of you has a grievance
against someone. Forgive as the Lord forgave you.*
—Colossians 3:13, NIV

Read: Matthew 18:21-35 and Acts 7:54-60

Every year, around the third week of November, my kids come home to
help decorate the tree. The night always starts with Chinese food and wraps
up with hot cocoa. But it's not just these bookends that make the night
special—it's everything in between. The memories we share while
unpacking those dusty boxes and carefully unwrapping each ornament take
us back to days gone by. And now, with grandchildren joining in, there's a
whole new layer of joy. Their excitement lights up the room as they hang
each ornament. Watching them feels like seeing the beauty and sparkle of
Christmas for the very first time.

You know, we can be a lot like those dusty boxes sometimes. Just like
we pack away the ornaments, we also pack away our emotions—our hurts,
disappointments, and even resentments. We push the pain aside, thinking
that if we box it up tightly enough, it'll stay out of sight and out of mind.
But here's the truth: the real burden isn't just what others have done to us;
it's what we carry when we refuse to let go and forgive.

Do you remember Jesus's words on the cross? Even in His greatest
suffering, He said, "Father, forgive them, for they do not know what they
are doing" (Luke 23:34). And then there's Stephen in Acts chapter 7. As
the stones rained down on him, he prayed, "Lord Jesus, receive my spirit."

Falling to his knees, he cried out, "Lord, do not hold this sin against them" (Acts 7:59-60). This was Stephen's heart, full of grace, choosing to live like Christ even in his final moments.

That's the kind of tender-heartedness we're called to show. But let's be honest—how many of us are willing to do that? To forgive before the sting of pain even begins to fade? And if we've held on to resentment for days, weeks, or even years, are we finally ready to let it go?

It's important to remember that forgiving someone doesn't mean we're excusing their behavior. Forgiveness is not saying that what happened was okay. Instead, it's about releasing the burden to God, trusting that He sees every wound and knows every injustice. When we forgive, we hand over our pain to the only One who can truly heal it. We're trusting God to be the just and righteous judge that He is. He sees the hurt and knows the heart, and He is faithful to fight for those He loves. Our part is to let go and trust Him to do what only He can do.

And here's something else—letting go doesn't just set others free; it sets us free too. When we decide to forgive, it's like opening a window in a room that's been shut up for too long. Fresh air flows in, and suddenly, the weight that once pressed down on us seems to lift. That's the beauty of God's grace: it doesn't just transform our circumstances; it transforms our hearts.

Today is a good day to dust off those old boxes, unpack the pain, and let the light of Christ shine in once again. Because I promise you, when you release the burden and let God take it, you'll find the peace and joy that's been hidden away for too long. And isn't that what we all truly long for? To live freely, to love deeply, and to let the grace of God shine through every part of our lives—just like the twinkling lights on our Christmas tree.

Today's Challenge:

Pray and ask God for the strength to forgive those who have wronged you, just as Jesus forgave from the cross. Then, take a tangible step toward letting go—whether it's a phone call, a prayer, or simply releasing it to the Lord.

What does Jesus' prayer for forgiveness on the cross (Luke 23:33-34) teach us about forgiving?

What two instructions does Romans 12:19 gives us for handling situations when we are wronged?

Show Compassion

Therefore, as God's chosen people, holy and dearly loved, clothe yourselves with compassion, kindness, humility, gentleness and patience.
—Colossians 3:12, NIV

Read: Luke 10:25-37 and Matthew 25:31-40 (NIV)

"C'mon," Michael will say, reaching over to grab a quilt from the living room basket, "put up your feet, and I'll tuck you in."

I'm a grandmother now, and I still lov

e being tucked in by Michael while we watch TV together. There's just something about it—the feeling of a warm blanket, a cup of hot cocoa, and a good Christmas movie. Especially one like *The Christmas Shoes*. Have you seen it? If not, let me give you some advice: grab a cozy blanket, a box of tissues, and settle in for a heartfelt story.

I won't give away too much, but let me tell you, this one pulls at your heartstrings in all the best ways. It's the kind of story that reminds us how small acts of kindness can have a huge impact, especially during the holidays. Trust me, you're going to need those tissues!

Watching that little boy with his tender heart got me thinking about compassion. Isn't that what the spirit of Christmas is all about? It's through selfless love and care that we reflect what Jesus has done for us. He came to us, not just as a symbol of love, but as an example of how to live with open, giving hearts—always ready to extend a hand.

In Matthew 22:37-39, Jesus tells us, "Love the Lord your God with all your heart, with all your soul, and with all your mind. This is the first and greatest commandment. And the second is like it: 'Love your neighbor as yourself.'" Now, being friendly and kind is one thing, but truly loving your neighbor goes deeper than "nice." It's more than a kind word or polite gesture; it's stepping into someone's story and caring from the heart.

Jesus gave us a powerful example in the parable of the Good Samaritan. In Luke 10:33, it says, "But a Samaritan, as he traveled, came where the man was; and when he saw him, he took pity on him." The word translated as "pity" here is from the Greek *splagchnizomai*, which means to be moved from the deepest part of yourself—an emotion that compels you to act. True compassion isn't just feeling sorry; it's letting that feeling lead you to act.

The word "compassion" comes from two Latin words: *com*, meaning "with," and *pati*, meaning "to suffer." To have compassion isn't just to observe someone's pain from afar—it's about coming alongside them, feeling their struggle, and choosing to be present. It's stepping into their shoes, much like that little boy did in *The Christmas Shoes*.

Isaiah 53:4 tells us that Jesus "bore our griefs and carried our sorrows." Jesus didn't see our suffering from afar; He entered into it fully. When we share in someone else's burdens, we reflect His love. This season, don't underestimate the power of small acts of kindness—a smile, a listening ear, or a helping hand. These moments can make a lasting impact, more than we realize.

As we celebrate Christmas, let's remember that compassion is at the heart of the season. Let's embrace the spirit of Christmas by walking alongside others, sharing in their joys, and carrying their burdens as He did for us. After all, the greatest gift we can give is to love others the way Christ first loved us.

Today's Challenge:

Look for ways to show compassion today—whether it's helping a neighbor, offering a word of encouragement, or simply listening to someone who needs to talk. Let your actions reflect the compassion of Christ and remember that even the smallest gesture can make a lasting impact on someone's day. Keep in mind Matthew 22:39—love your neighbor as yourself.

What does it mean to "love your neighbor as yourself" in the context of Luke 10:25-37?

What are some specific ways (big or small) you can show compassion and kindness to others this Christmas season?

Day 25

Offer Kindness

Therefore, as God's chosen people, holy and dearly loved, clothe yourselves with compassion, kindness, humility, gentleness and patience.
—Colossians 3:12, NIV

Read: Ruth 1&2 and Colossians 3:12-17

I read a quote the other day that said, "Being a family means you are a part of something wonderful. It means you will love and be loved for the rest of your life, no matter what." —Lisa Weed.

I don't know about you, but that's certainly been true in my life. Friends have come and gone over the years. Neighbors have moved here and there. Coworkers I once shared so much with have long forgotten my name. But through it all, family has remained the one constant—especially my sisters.

These are the girls I spent countless Christmases with, celebrated birthdays, and ate the same meals around the kitchen table. We shared the same parents, and sometimes, we even shared the same bed. We drank cherry Kool-Aid while watching *The Brady Bunch* and *Columbo* together. We played endless rounds of Monopoly, baked cakes in our Easy Bake Ovens, and dreamed of one day finishing our Doodle Art. Family is special like that. It's a bond that's unique and unlike any other.

As I thought about this today, I noticed something interesting— "kindness" and "kin" share the same root word. I never really thought about that before, but they do. And maybe it's because real kindness is about treating people like family.

Think back to Ruth and Naomi for a moment. Remember what Ruth said to her mother-in-law? "Where you go I will go, and where you stay I will stay. Your people will be my people and your God my God" (Ruth 1:16, NIV). Ruth's kindness wasn't driven by duty. It came from a place of deep love and loyalty. She could have chosen the easier path and returned to her own family, but instead, she chose the sacrificial one. Ruth's story shows us that kindness is more than just being nice; it's about stepping into someone else's life with a heart ready to love and support, no matter the cost.

Paul paints a beautiful picture of what kindness looks like in Colossians 3:12: "Therefore, as God's chosen people, holy and dearly loved, clothe yourselves with compassion, kindness, humility, gentleness, and patience." Family teaches us so much about these qualities, doesn't it? It's where we first learn how to forgive, how to show patience, and how to extend grace. These are reflections of Christ that make family bonds so strong, but they aren't meant to be kept within our families—they're meant to be shared with everyone around us.

Anyone can wrap a gift and put it under the tree. But if we really want to embrace the spirit of kindness this Christmas, our gifts need to come from the heart. So this year, let's give in a way that reflects the sacrificial love of Jesus—gifts of kindness, compassion, mercy, forgiveness, and grace. These are the kinds of gifts that go beyond the wrapping paper and bows— they touch hearts, they make an impact, and they remind us of the love we've already received from our Savior.

Let's make it our mission this season to be "kin" to everyone around us—treating them with the same love, patience, and kindness that we give to our families. That's the spirit of Christmas.

Today's Challenge:

Focus on practicing kindness in small, intentional ways today. Whether it's sending an encouraging note, giving someone extra patience, or doing something thoughtful without being asked, let kindness lead your actions. Remember, kindness often goes unnoticed, but its impact is felt deeply.

What are some specific ways you can show sacrificial kindness, like Ruth did with Naomi, to others this Christmas?

What does Paul mean in Colossians 3:10 when he says we have "put on the new self?" And how is this "new self" being renewed?

Nurture Relationships

Be devoted to one another in love. Honor one another
above yourselves. —Romans 12:10, NIV

Read: 1 Samuel 18-20

A few years back, I bought some cream-colored shag carpets—the perfect fit for our dining and living room areas. They looked beautiful, soft, and cozy, especially with the warm glow of the Christmas tree lights. I wanted an elegant touch, something that would make our home feel festive yet peaceful during the holidays. Since we didn't spend much time in those rooms, I hoped they might stay that way for years. And for the most part, they did. With the kids grown, we spent most of our time in the family room, and the cream shag remained pristine.

But I didn't anticipate the damage one little dog could do—especially one sick little dog who had gotten into some food he shouldn't have. One afternoon, I came home after picking up the kids from school. After carrying in the groceries and slipping off my shoes, I was shocked by what I found. Our pug had been sick, and if you know anything about dogs, you know they're always drawn to the carpet when they're not feeling well. The mess was everywhere—from the living room sofa to the dining room table, with several stops in between. Any other type of carpet might have survived, but white shag didn't. Looking back, I can admit that maybe choosing white shag wasn't the best idea.

Michael, on the other hand, has always been wiser than me when it comes to practical choices. Ten years later, the braided rug in his office still looks just as good as the day he bought it. The classic style of a braided rug has grown on me over the years. They add warmth to a room, but more importantly, they're built to last—they can handle the wear and tear of life.

Thinking about those braided rugs reminds me of what it means to have strong, lasting relationships. Ecclesiastes 4:12 tells us, "A cord of three strands is not quickly broken." What holds true for a strong braided cord also holds true for our lives. Our connections—whether with family, friends, or God—are stronger when they are intertwined, when there are multiple strands holding us up.

As we approach Christmas, I'm reminded that nurturing relationships is one of the ways we truly embrace the spirit of the season. Like the braided rug, the bonds we share with those around us—family, friends, and most importantly, God—are what keep us grounded. Woven together, these bonds form a strength that no single strand could achieve alone.

Whether it's in our marriage, friendships, or the love we have for our families, when God is at the center, He is the strand that holds us together and sustains us through the ups and downs of life. This holiday season, as we gather around the tree, exchange gifts, and share meals, let's nurture these bonds. Let's be intentional about weaving God into every relationship, knowing that with Him in the mix, our connections endure.

When we invest in these relationships, we reflect the true spirit of Christmas. It's not about having perfect decorations or spotless cream carpets—it's about letting love grow, embracing the mess, and holding tight to the people woven into our lives.

Today's Challenge:

Take a moment today to nurture one of your important relationships. It could be as simple as sharing a kind word, sending an encouraging message, or spending uninterrupted time with a loved one. Reflect on how God strengthens our connections when we make Him the center. Let's be intentional about weaving His love into every bond, allowing our relationships to reflect His grace, especially during this Christmas season.

Speaking metaphorically, why is a strand of three cords stronger than one?

What are some ways you can nurture the bonds of your relationships to make them stronger this holiday season?

Focus on Others

Whatever you do, work at it with all your heart, as working
for the Lord, not for human masters, since you know that you will receive an
inheritance from the Lord as a reward. It is the Lord Christ
you are serving. —Colossians 3:23-24, NIV

Read: Isaiah 58:6-10, Philippians 2:1-8

One of our favorite Christmas traditions is something we call "Serve in Secret." Michael and I have been doing this for years, and it has always been a highlight of our holiday season. Anytime we thought we couldn't afford it or got too busy to make it happen, we ended up wishing we could start the season over and do it anyway. So we commit each year to quietly bless someone God has placed on our hearts.

One year, we surprised a family with a Christmas tree and ornaments. Another time, we bought groceries for someone going through a rough patch. And one year, Michael went above and beyond to pick out beautiful gifts for a young girl and her mom. I was ready to settle on practical clothes, but Michael insisted on the prettiest dress in the store—and, of course, a stuffed animal to go with it too.

I feel like I've let you in on a little secret here, but the real joy isn't in the recognition. It's knowing that, in some small way, we've brought a little light into someone's life. This tradition is close to our hearts because of Jesus' words in Matthew 6:3-4: "But when you give to the needy, do not let your left hand know what your right hand is doing, so that your giving may be in secret. Then your Father, who sees what is done in secret, will reward you."

Serving in secret lets us be humble vessels of God's love, without any expectation of praise. The reward is in the giving itself—in knowing that we're sharing His love, one act of kindness at a time.

Jesus gave us the perfect example of focusing on others. Though He was King, He came to earth and took on the form of a servant (Philippians 2:7). He knelt to wash the disciples' feet (John 13:4-8) and said, "For even the Son of Man did not come to be served, but to serve, and to give his life as a ransom for many" (Mark 10:45). If Jesus humbled Himself in service, how much more should we follow His lead?

In a season that so easily becomes focused on ourselves—with gifts, food, and the comforts of the holiday—let's take time to focus on others. Maybe that means helping with dishes, bringing a meal to someone, offering a ride to church, baking treats for a neighbor, shoveling a sidewalk, or volunteering at a local shelter. These small, simple acts can make a big difference.

As Paul writes in Colossians, "Whatever you do, work at it with all your heart, as working for the Lord, not for human masters, since you know that you will receive an inheritance from the Lord as a reward. It is the Lord Christ you are serving" (Colossians 3:23-24).

So this Christmas, let's choose to focus on others, following the example of our Savior—giving from the heart and trusting that God will use even our smallest acts of kindness for His glory. That's where the true joy of the season is found.

Today's Challenge:

Choose one person—a family member, friend, or neighbor—and do something kind for them without expecting anything in return, and without revealing who did it. It could be something simple like shoveling snow off their driveway, dropping off some baking, or writing an anonymous note of encouragement. The idea is to focus on others without recognition, knowing your reward comes from God.

How does the idea of "serving in secret" resonate with you? Can you think of an opportunity to serve someone this week without expecting recognition?

When you think about Jesus serving others, how does that shape the way you want to serve those around you this Christmas?

Be Mindful of Others

Do nothing out of selfish ambition or vain conceit. Rather, in humility value others above yourselves, not looking to your own interests but each of you to the interests of the others. —Philippians 2:3-4, NIV

Read: Luke 10:38-42 and Galatians 6

So, we went camping with the family last summer... but I have to admit, one of my friends would call it "cheating" if I used the word "camping." The cabins we stayed in had all the amenities—showers, television, internet, and even comfy beds. I know, I know... How did I manage to make it through the weekend, right?

While we may not be by an ocean here in Manitoba, we're blessed with two large lakes. Nestled along one of them is a special place for our family— the beautiful Hecla Island. We used to take our kids there when they were little, and now we get the joy of bringing our grandkids. It's become a tradition—having lunch at the Little Viking Restaurant before climbing the steps of the Gull Harbor Lighthouse. The lighthouse isn't in use anymore, but at one time, it guided boats safely through the rough waters of Lake Winnipeg.

The beautiful thing about a lighthouse is that it doesn't shine to get noticed; it shines to guide boats safely home. Its light keeps them from danger and offers a sense of security in the midst of a storm.

In the same way, we're called to stand firm and be mindful of others. Hearts can be heavy at Christmas, and let's face it—the hustle and bustle of the season comes with its fair share of stress. While it's a season that should be joyful and bright, it often illuminates darkness and sorrow for some. But here's the thing: mindfulness isn't just about seeing a need; it's about stepping in and acting with love, just like Jesus did when He touched the sick, fed the hungry, and welcomed the outcasts. He didn't simply notice a need—He moved toward people with compassion, offering healing and hope.

If we hope to be mindful, we have to be present. That means putting our phones aside, turning off the TV, and slowing down long enough to sit with others. It's about pausing our own agenda for the sake of someone else. We see this beautifully illustrated in the story of Mary and Martha in Luke chapter 10. The Bible tells us that Martha was "distracted" with all of the preparations she had to tend to. Unlike her sister, Mary sat at Jesus' feet, fully present and listening. When Martha asked Jesus, "Lord, don't you care that my sister has left me to do the work by myself? Tell her to help me!" He gently pointed out that Mary had chosen what was better—she was mindful of Christ.

This year, as we're preparing for Christmas, let's remember the gift that's been given to us. Mindful of our deepest need for salvation, Jesus left the comforts of heaven behind and chose the way of the cross. By following His example of mindfulness, we're not just embracing the spirit of Christmas—we're living it out in a way that brings glory to Him.

Today's Challenge:

Choose one moment today to be fully present with someone. Whether it's a family member, a friend, or even a stranger, set aside distractions like your phone or other tasks. Listen intently, offer a kind word, or simply sit with someone. Carry this practice into the rest of the Christmas season.

Throughout His ministry, Jesus was mindful of those in need, stepping in with love and compassion. What are some specific ways you can act on the needs of those around you this Christmas?

How can we, like Mary, "choose what is better" this Christmas?

Made in the USA
Monee, IL
15 November 2024

70196837R00077